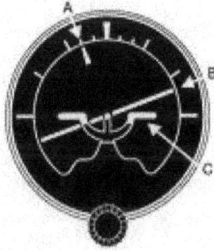

Aviation Faith Series

VOLUME I

By Blessings Storehouse Ministries,
Author: Tarja A. Newman

ATTITUDES

that get you

RESULTS

Table of Contents

Foreword

It is with great pleasure that I write this foreword. During the time I have known the author her love of God and dedication to not only, believing Jesus' Word and all His teachings, but also, living those teachings in her daily walk has impressed me. The approach she has taken in this work to develop an easily comprehendible analogy about one of the most important subjects facing each of us as we deal with the complexities of today's society is fascinating. It really demonstrates the reality that God's principals for our behavior are the same principals He established for everything in creation.

If we look closely at the bible we find that attitude is found in virtually every verse in the bible either in the positive or negative sense or as an explanation of the consequences of one of the first two. I pray that many people will be touched greatly by this work.

Most reverend +Roger Smyzer, Abp, JD, DVM,

Ukrainian Autocephalous National-Orthodox Church
of America and Europe, Blessing of Kiev

Acknowledgments and Thanks

Because being thankful is a major part of wisdom and receiving from God, I first of all want to acknowledge and thank Him for living in me and being THE SOURCE of all wisdom and revelation. I want to give credit to the Father, Son and the Holy Spirit for His leading and opening of my eyes and heart to see and hear what He has to say.

I also want to thank here the people that were a great influence and support for putting this book together. First of all, I want to thank my husband Nick whom I admire and respect. He has been my great support both in life and in writing this book. He has also shared in on the Wisdom Nuggets. I love you!

Thank you also to my mom and dad, Elina and Juhani. Without you, I wouldn't exist. You always encouraged us and gave us the freedom to reach high. Thank you for the faith and belief you instilled in us and the sacrifices you made on our behalf that we may pursue our dreams.

My brother Kari, aka "Kuja", whose passion has always been music, you have proven that when you have a dream, you can achieve anything in life when you don't give up, but pursue. You are one of a kind in your industry and I am so proud of you.

Otilia, my mother-in-law, and Rodica, my sister-in-law, you prayed with my husband to be and your son and brother for his future wife and claimed my salvation for me before you even knew me. For that I am eternally grateful.

Pastor Stan and your family, you are the reason why this book began. Your teaching of Attitude inspired this book and I thank you.

Arch Bishop Roger Smyzer, Minister, Attorney and a personal friend, you have been instrumental in so many ways in our lives and in writing this book, more than you'll ever know.

Thank you also to Airborne Systems Flight School, where I have the privilege of working with awesome colleagues and students of Aviation. You all have been a blessing in my life beyond words. There are many more, who have been influential in my life, too many to mention here. You know who you are and I am blessed to have you in my life.

Last but not least, I want to thank Michael and Stefan Strasser from Chicken Wings Comics who graciously allowed me to use their material in this book. Please visit them at www.chickenwingscomics. com for a lot more fun and laughter. You'll find that there are a lot more lessons learned there as well.

Revelations from Aviation for Everyday Life

Right Attitudes, Trust and
Willingness to Obey

Whether you rise or fall is based on your Attitude!

CHAPTER ONE

Wisdom Nugget #1

Faith works by
Love and the Attitude
of Thanksgiving
breaks through
every wall of
bondage.

CHAPTER ONE

Basic Instruments

Attitude Instrument

There are a lot of things in life that relates to flying and vice versa. Many principles that I teach in aviation also applies to life. It is really amazing to see how many things have been in the Bible all along, well before flight for humans was ever invented.

What got me looking at the relationship between the principles of flight and life in general and how this relates to scripture is my pastor, Stan Moore from North Miami, FL. As he started to teach about attitude some years ago, I came to realize that there are many commonalities between lessons of life and flight, and all of it has been in the scripture all along.

I am a very visual person as I am sure many of you are. When I teach, I try to keep it very simple. If at all possible I attempt to make it visual, just the way my pastor does. He and I both come from a coaching background and I believe we are both bringing this into our teaching style. As a coach, our pastor often has us repeat words after him. In other words, he is helping us to get it by rehearsing the scripture actively ourselves instead of just passively listening. Every so often he will come up with pictures and visuals that relate to the message and the truth that is being portrayed. This will make us all capture the vision more easily and more importantly, understand it.

The same way in flying, making a connection between what you are attempting to learn and something else that you already know and relate to is a great way to get understanding about new subject, or even a new revelation about something you though you already understood. This, I found was happening to me regarding to understanding the importance of attitude.

We have all heard that attitude is everything. I don't know how many of us really understand the reality of it, but visualize this. You are flying an airplane and you cannot see outside. You are flying totally based on the indications of the instruments. You have what is called an Attitude Indicator in the cockpit that tells you not only which side is up and which side is down, but it also indicates a climbing, descending and a banking attitude of your airplane. Correctly adjusted it will tell you when you are flying straight and level as it has a miniature airplane that moves against the horizon behind it, so you can tell if you have a nose low, nose up or a level attitude.

You have to trust the instruments, being that you cannot see outside and what you feel may not be the truth. Often little bumps and/or head movements can create an illusion that you are climbing, turning or descending, when that is not true at all. You've just got to trust what those instruments are telling you or you may be the cause of an unusual attitude of the airplane and the reason for it coming down. It's all about the correct attitude.

You'll understand the importance of the attitude if you know this one thing about airplanes, that the plane cannot keep increasing its nose up attitude higher and higher forever. There is such a thing what we call a "critical angle of attack" at which point the plane stops flying and the nose drops down once you reach this critical attitude. When this happens, the plane will come down whether you like it or not. How this relates to life is the same thing that happens when someone is high minded and has a lofty attitude. Eventually that person will come down. This, too, is scriptural. In Proverbs 16:18 it tells us that "Pride goes before destruction and a haughty spirit before a fall".

The interesting part of it all is that whether your attitude is too high or too low, either way you are coming down. See, in airplanes, just like in life, attitude is everything. If you set the nose of the airplane too low, meaning you have a lousy attitude, eventually you are going to hit the ground.

This may also happen if your attitude reaches the critical nose high attitude at which it is impossible for the plane to fly. The plane will drop its nose and start heading down. However, if your attitude is just right, you can climb higher and higher (up to the airplane's limits of course) and you can reach new horizons.

Turn Coordinator

There's another part of the right attitude and that's keeping it coordinated. For that we use "Turn and Slip Indicator", or a "Turn Coordinator". When you are coordinated, you are balanced. The dangers of not staying balanced is that an uncoordinated flight could end up in a spin, a steep spiral or even a nose dive. That will, however, only happen if you reach that critical attitude we call a "critical angle of attack". So, in other words, should you have the critical attitude and at the same time slip or skid, you could spin down, end up in a steep spiral or a nose dive. This could be deadly, unless you have time to correct this attitude before it's too late. The only difference between spinning down and spiraling down is the speed. Spinning is a stalled condition and steep spiral is practically a turning nose dive.

I have only experienced a nose dive once, when a student put me into one several years ago during a spin training session. You are only required to go through the spin training and actual spin and recovery from it if you are going to become a Flight Instructor. For any other pilot license you'll just need to thoroughly understand what could get you into one and know how to avoid a spin, spiral, stall, nose dive etc., and also how to recover in the event of any of that ever happening inadvertently.

Fortunately, for spin training you have a lot of altitude beneath you and have time to recover. However, you should never attempt to get into one of those nose dives or steep spirals no matter how high you are! The speed limits for the airplane can be exceeded in a split second and there is no fast recovery, just a deliberate, meticulous and careful moving of controls in order to return to normal flight. And, after that, there's a careful inspection of the airplane that survived with you. If you try to level the wings of the plane for a normal flight too fast, again, you could exceed structural limits of the airplane (and I really do like to have the wings and all other flying surfaces still attached to the airplane when I land.)

There is, however, one good reason that we would want a plane to stall. You see, when a plane stalls, it is releasing the load off the wings that it is trying to carry. So, if you would rapidly approach that critical angle of attack by pulling the nose of the airplane too high up, you would rapidly also increase the load that the wings are supporting. It's what we call the G-load factor. In other words, the actual weight load could double, triple and quadruple or more by the sudden changes in attitude.

Instead of just breaking the wings off the airplane under the tremendous load, the plane will release the load off by stalling. By doing this, the attitude of the airplane recovers back to where it can fly again besides keeping its wings. So it is the planes natural way to try to recover itself.

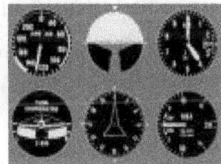

Other Basic Instruments

There are other instruments that are confirming the attitude of the airplane and the direction you are moving. Among them are "Altimeter", "Airspeed Indicator", "Vertical Speed Indicator" we call VSI and a "Directional Gyro" i.e. DG, which is a Heading Indicator.

Altimeter tells your altitude, usually above Sea Level. Here in Florida, that's practically the altitude above the ground. In a stall, a spin, a spiral, a nose dive or any low attitude, the altimeter will confirm that you are indeed approaching the ground by showing ever decreasing altitude.

VSI will join in this indication and will tell you how fast you are approaching the ground. It will indicate a descend in feet per minute. At this point your airspeed would also be increasing, confirming a nose low attitude.

Finally, your DG, Directional Gyro, which is your heading indicator would show you if you are turning while you are descending. In a spin or a steep spiral this would be the case. If something does not match the picture and confirm what the rest of the instruments are reading, it may be faulty.

So also in life, there may be many indications for the situations we go through. In any case, it is God's Word we should rely on for every indication to confirm it is true what we perceive. Remember, there are the facts and then there is the truth and they don't always match. You choose what you believe. In the case of flying the airplane, the fact may be that you may feel that you are upside down or turning, but the truth is you are flying straight and level based on the instruments.

So, if all the indications match each other, the indication is true. The same is true, if what you perceive in life matches God's Word. TRUST THE INDICATIONS OF GOD'S WORD!

CHAPTER TWO

Wisdom Nugget #2

Wisdom
comes through
understanding
knowledge.

CHAPTER TWO

Navigational Instruments

VOR, RMI, HSI and NDB

There are some basic navigational instruments in most airplanes. VOR stands for Very High frequency Omni-directional Range. VOR is an electronic navigation equipment in which the flight deck instrument, called VOR, identifies a signal that radiates from a VOR station on the ground. We call this signal a radial from a ground based VOR station. These "radials" are signaled from the VOR stations to all directions (360 degrees) around it, therefore the name 'Omni-directional".

On a VOR instrument, you can select which radial you would like to navigate to and it will give you basic information as to the direction of the radial. You can also identify which radial you are on at your current position. Once the pilot identifies which radial the plane is from a VOR station, you can tell if you are east, west, north or south from a particular station. Therefore, you can pinpoint your exact location with the help of just two VOR's and navigate with the help of VOR's to your destination. Each VOR station has its own frequency that can be selected on the receiver in the airplane, much like you would select a TV channel or a radio station.

ADF is Automatic Direction Finder and receives low and medium frequency signal from a Non-Directional Beacon called NDB for short. The one difference between and NDB and a VOR is that instead of calling the signals "radials from", the ADF has "bearings to" the station.

Each NDB has a frequency, just like a VOR that can be selected on the ADF "dial" in the airplane. The

ADF "needle" is a pointer on the instrument that always points at the station which is selected on the dial. It's kind of like the Holy Spirit who always points to Jesus. You can follow the head of the "needle" right to the station or the "tail of the needle" away from the station in the direction you want to navigate.

RMI is a Radio Magnetic Indicator, which functions much the same way than ADF needle, except that it always points at a VOR station. So, an RMI then receives those high frequency signals from a VOR station and an ADF receives those low and medium frequency signals from an NDB. RMI also combines a magnetic compass with an ADF or a VOR and shows the magnetic heading the aircraft is flying while pointing to the station.

HSI is a Horizontal Situation Indicator that also combines the heading indicator. But, HSI displays a needle that we call CDI, a Course Deviation Needle, which will immediately tell the pilot if he is deviating off course. All you need to do to stay on course is to keep the needle centered and follow it to the left of right, if it moves, to stay on course.

Global Positioning System

More technologically advanced airplanes have instruments that will even show you if you are tracking in the right direction. This is called Global Positioning System, or GPS for short. FMS is another name for the basically same thing and stands for Flight Management System. In both systems, you can input your flight plan into the system and it then directs you on the right path. Since both systems basically operate in the same manner, I will simply talk about GPS referring to both systems.

Whether or not you input your flight plan into the system, the GPS display will show you the direction you are tracking. If you do have a flight plan in the system, it now also tells you if you are tracking along its path or if you are off course. Should you be off course, it will show you the direction to go to return back on course in order to land at your destination.

In life, you can "manage your flight through life" or "position yourself" by checking your progress in relation to God's instructions in the Word. The Word of God really functions the same way. If you pay attention to it, it will let you know if you are on the right track and also shows you the way to go. All you have to do is pay attention to it and that small still voice inside of you.

These optional instruments can be added to basically any airplane. Even *you* can develop *your* "instruments of the Spirit" by meditating on the Word and spending time with Him in order to hear from Him and therefore remain in the right path. The first thing to start with, if you haven't done so yet, is to add Global Positioning System, the infilling of the Holy Spirit, within you. With His help you can position yourself where *you* need to be to fulfill your purpose. No matter what instruments God wants to use in your life to receive His instructions, be it the Bible, a Word through a minister or a revelation knowledge directly received by you, you still need the receiver to receive. The Holy Spirit in you is the instrument that enables you to receive from Him all that He has for you. The best part is that this instrument is free! Jesus paid the price when He died and sent His Holy Spirit for you here on earth. All you have to do is accept this free gift from Him and let Him install it!

Trusting the Instruments

Finally, I want to talk about the importance of the attitude and how one can maintain it in an airplane. If you are in the cockpit, flying around with no visual references outside, it's like your life's circumstances that seem to block your view to what's really going on. Don't let that distract you! Just trust the instruments. This, in life is the Word of God. What does it say? Act based on it, not how you feel. Storms of life are there trying to upset your attitude, much the same way like flying an airplane through a storm, that storm is doing its best to upset the airplane. If you let your feelings take over, you are letting the storm win. You've got to maintain control of that attitude or the end result could be hazardous.

When you are flying through some rough weather in life, watch your attitude! This principle alone has saved many lives in an airplane - and not trusting the attitude indicator and other instruments confirming the unusual attitude has caused many not so fortunate results. Often this is the case, when one is on denial and cannot believe that something is indeed happening. For example, you may be flying straight and level, but you feel that you are turning! But, because of some little "bumps on the road" (or the airway) made you feel that you weren't flying just right, you made a wrong input and now you put yourself in an unusual attitude, perhaps a nose dive. In other words, you yourself upset your attitude with just a little help from your surroundings.

Remember, rough weather does not last forever. If you are finding yourself in a low attitude, "down in the dumps", you can't allow yourself to stay there! You must encourage yourself in the Lord, trust in His Word! In aviation, this would be adjusting your attitude in order to recover.

When you do encounter a rough ride, however, don't hesitate to ask for help. There's Air Traffic Controller out there that can see the weather on their radar and give you the best direction to go to. They are able to help you to deviate and avoid the worst conditions that you could be facing without the extra help. There are times, though, that it may be impossible to avoid the weather all together. Those are the times when you just have to go through and accept all the help that's available to you.

This has happened to me once or twice. One time we had launched to our destination, which was perfectly in the clear, but the weather was moving in onto our departure airport. Once we took off and had departed, the weather started to close in a lot faster than forecasted. Not only did it close the airport behind us, so there was no turning back, but the weather also surrounded us from all around. So, the bottom line was, the only option left for us was to go through. We asked for the best vector through the line of weather as there were no openings around it.

When you do have to endure the rough ride, the controller is also able tell you how long it may be until you'll come out on the other side. This was the case on that day and we were informed to just keep the heading they gave us and the rough ride was going to be over in just 7 miles.

The Air Traffic Controller (ATC) is out there to help you, just like God is there to direct you. All you need to do is ask, listen and obey. So, the key is to keep in touch with the Air Traffic Controller. Keep the communications open.

Sometimes you may have a radar on board the aircraft and you may be able to see it yourself which is the best direction to proceed and which way to avoid. This is just like having the Holy Spirit guiding you in the affairs of life. Holy Spirit is really like a combination of an on board Radar, Navigation and Communication System. He is the connection with the Air Traffic Control and He is also the Navigational Signal. And, just like Radar, He can see the things that lie ahead of you and warn you of things to come, so you can avoid the dangers while inside your circumstances.

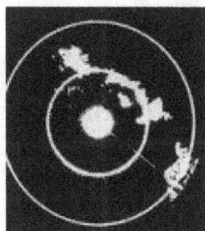

CHAPTER THREE

Wisdom Nugget #3

Stay steady on
course. Even a turtle
reaches his destination
before a rabbit when
he stays steady
on course.

CHAPTER THREE

Preflight Planning

CHICKEN WINGS™

BY MICHAEL AND STEFAN STRASSER

THAT'S FUNNY. I DON'T RECOGNIZE ANY OF THIS. I THINK WE'RE LOST!

LET'S FLY TO THAT LANDMARK OVER THERE!

ON SECOND THOUGHT... THIS ALL *DOES* LOOK FAMILIAR ...SOMEHOW.

CHECK IT OUT! I'VE NEVER SEEN AN F-16 THIS CLOSE BEFORE! AWESOME!!

YOU KNOW, I THINK THIS COULD BE A BAD SIGN.

www.chickenwingscomics.com

You should also never take off, until you have done a through preflight planning. This includes pulling all the resources together to make sure that not only the flight can be completed, but that it can be accomplished safely. You check the airplane that it is airworthy, the weather is suitable, complete weight and balance calculations for the airplane, so you can be assured of a controllable and manageable airplane and create a flight plan among other important things. In other words, you get the "big picture". You prepare your way and plan for the upcoming circumstances. You even prepare for the unexpected, so that hopefully nothing can take you by surprise, like an emergency, because you were prepared.

If you ever got yourself in trouble because of your decisions or lack of planning, in aviation you can always ask for help from ATC and also the Flight Service Station. They are there to serve YOU. In an emergency you can tell THEM what you need to do. The same way, in your own life situations, whether or not you were the one who caused the problem while navigating through the airways of life, you always have available to you God, the Holy Spirit and His angels to serve you. You can command the angels on your behalf to do what you need to get done. They, too, are here to serve YOU.

No matter what, even in life, it is better to prepare when it is calm, before any rising storm. Preparing in a storm is a whole lot harder and perhaps too late.

Talking about planning, before each flight you must be totally prepared and aware of anything that could affect the safety or any other aspect of the flight. You must prepare so you can increase your chances of getting to your destination. So it is also in life. How many times do we see people have this 'just wait and see attitude' and nothing ever gets accomplished? Someone once said that grave yard is full of dreams not reached, songs unsung and books never written. I hope that in some way I may be used of God through this writing to encourage you to never have that attitude, but instead to go forward to fulfill the dreams in your heart. May you be inspired to move on with your dreams the same way God inspired me.

This happened to me when I was listening to someone about his revelation how God created this world and all that is within it and how He started with the Vision of the end result first. God then re-winded all the way to the beginning and started building from there towards the end result that He had already seen. So, He had already been to the end result and seen the end. That is His vision. Now, He simply moved Himself all the way to the beginning, i.e. He "unwound" the vision to its foundation and started building on it. And, here we are, all of us in His plan still moving towards the final plan of God. all of us are part of it whether or not we see it at the moment.

What inspired me about this teaching is the truth that if you do what God did from the very beginning you, too, will be clear on how to get to where you're going! So, start with your destination, your goal, your vision. Where do you see yourself going? Where do you desire to go to? What is it that you feel passionately that you are to do? Those are the seeds of the vision God has put inside of you! Now, envision the end result and see all the parts all neatly fit together. Then break it down to smaller pieces and smaller pieces, until the pieces are small enough for you to start putting the big picture in place.

Build on that until you have the complete picture and then build it bigger! Go for it and dream big! God never dreamed small and neither should you. After all, we are His body and we are a big part of His vision. Now do your part.

Getting to Your Destination

So it all starts with the preflight planning, but what about the practical part? The following is the information how to get to your destination when the weather conditions will prevent you to "fly by sight". In other words, when there is a need to "go by faith" and fly by trusting the instruments, when the outside visual references cannot be seen and you need the help of the Air Traffic Controller to clear your way to your destination. That's when there is no way you could do it on your own.

When you first start off from your departure airport, you need to announce your intentions, especially when an airport has a control tower. That means that the control tower is in charge and in control of every move that takes place in his airspace (and "ground space").

In all controlled airports you will have a recording of what the current weather and other conditions of the field are. We call this ATIS (Automatic Terminal Information Service). You will need to listen to this information before you proceed to do anything. This will give you the pertinent information that would affect your departure from that airport.

After you have acquired that information you'll contact "Clearance Delivery". Most of the larger airports have Clearance Delivery frequency as they need to orchestrate all the traffic departing from that particular airspace. They will give you your personal clearance of how to get to your destination. You will need to copy that clearance word for word as it is your step by step instruction how you are to proceed to where you are going. This would also be your first indication of how to continue your journey should there be a case of lost communication in your route. You would simply follow the last directions given to you by the controller.

After you have received your instructions, you will contact Ground Control. Since you are still on the ground, Ground Controller will be directing you on your way to the right runway in preparation for take-off. They will most likely tell you to stay on their frequency until *you* tell *them* that *you are ready* to proceed for takeoff phase. At that time they will coordinate you with the next controller for takeoff in order to sequence you into all the other traffic on their way to their own destinations.

Once the way is clear and there is a good timing for your departure, the Ground Controller tells you to contact the Tower for your departure. The Tower will be giving you the specific headings that you are to follow to keep you clear of other traffic as well as obstacles. You are to read back all clearances and directions so that the controller will know you have copied the instructions correctly and are indeed flying the direction that he intents you to go for the moment. Let's say that the direction the controller instructs you to fly after takeoff is West and you instead reply "East", he will immediately correct you and demand the correct response and action. He is only doing this to protect you and others. After all, you could be flying head on against other traffic that you would not see coming your way, if the directions are not followed carefully. The controller is really trying to keep everyone from danger and from making mistakes by confirming you truly understand and are going to comply with directions given.

Once you leave the airport area, the Tower Controller is going to give you yet another frequency to contact the Departure Control. You will simply check in as they are expecting your call and they will continue giving you headings and altitudes that you are to fly. So, you are moving from one phase to another continually and you will never want to be out of touch with the Air Traffic Controller. It is all a finely orchestrated sequence.

Also, once you are airborne, be quick to follow directions as you are now moving a lot faster than you were when you were on the ground. If the need arises for you to change course, be it for weather or for any other looming danger, the Air Traffic Controller will contact you to let you know of a new direction to follow. Be quick to obey as it is to your benefit.

As the flight progresses and your altitudes change, you will be constantly given new frequencies to stay in touch with the Controller. Although the frequencies change along the way and phases and locations of flight are changing, the directions are all designed to get you to your destination safely. So, just like in life and with God, we are moving from one phase to another throughout our lives, from Glory to Glory, the *frequencies* that you will develop to hear will change as you move from one phase to another and from one level to another. But, your destination is still the same, designed by God.

If you tune your ear to hear the directions and copy and follow them to the tee, you will get to your destination safely with the help of the Traffic Controller, which is the Holy Spirit. But, unless you keep moving and progressing forward, there's no need for new frequencies.

So, the choice is yours. You can follow the directions

to the tee so that you may proceed to the next phase of flight. Or, you might be stuck on the ground if you are not ready, nor allowed to take off if you are not able to follow directions. Develop a good listening ear and then follow the directions and you, too, will reach your destination designed for you.

Approaching the Destination

When you are approaching the destination, you have to get ready with all the appropriate information relating to the arrival airport. This includes getting the ATIS information, which will inform you about the weather, the runways in use and other important information, so you can plan on how to enter the airport area. You will also receive the information on what kind of instrument approach is in use, so you can set up appropriately and be ready as early as possible.

Constantly vigilant for any system malfunction
the Captain scans the overhead panel as the co-pilot
checks the window heat system with his forehead —
at 03:00 pilots can't be too careful.....

Everything is preparation. If you are not prepared, you will be behind every step. Even God in His mercy would not let you approach your destination unless you are ready for the next step. How often are we waiting for God to move and we haven't done what He has asked of us in the first place? This is all preparation that God is asking us to do so we can be prepared to move on to the next step.

It would be dangerous for a pilot to attempt to start an approach to an airport and not having set up the correct frequencies on the navigational instruments. He would not be receiving the correct information unless he was set up first with the correct input in the system. Not only would you not end up at your destination, but this could be a matter of life and death in some more dangerous territory, like mountainous areas for example. Yet how many of us have persisted in moving one direction in our lives and clearly God has tried to tell us not yet, or not you.

Perhaps you had *your* thoughts and *your* goals and it was *your* idea to continue in one direction, when God was directing you to change your direction, to move into another area. I certainly have done that in the past at least twice. Both of them relates to flying.

One of the times I had audacious goals, particularly relating to a business I was running at the time. When God wanted to change my direction back into flying, I rebelled thinking I thought I was supposed to be the financier of the Kingdom of God and I had planned for that business to be the way to do so. Besides, I had not been flying for approximately 8 years! It took Him 3 months to completely change my heart and I was back in flying. Once He did, He said to me that "What once was dead is now resurrected and therefore it cannot be killed again". I never forgot that.

As far as financing the Gospel, I still think I am also going to do that as it has been the desire of my heart from the very beginning, but I do trust that God has His way of doing that and He will direct me how I can be part of it.

The second time a similar situation took place was two years after my flying career with the airlines had come to an end. I had again resorted to running my own business when God started to give me clear directions to take my resume to a particular Flight School. I always loved flight instructing, but when He asked me to bring my resume to flight instruct, I was questioning God - out of fear really - since I had not flown for some time. Not only had I not flown for two years, but I had not flown a *small* airplane for 7 years. How could I jump in and teach? However, I did remember what He had told me the first time He brought aviation back into my life that this aviation thing could not be killed in my life any more.

After I had delayed for two weeks my obedience of simply bringing my resume to where He directed me to go I finally did so. When I did, I was informed that I should have stopped by two weeks ago! That's when they had just hired two flight instructors, but they'd love to have me and said they would call me as soon as there was another opening. Well they did and there I am even now at the time of this writing.

So, if you want to get to your destination, you've got to tune in to the right frequency and identify that you got the right one by listening to the Morse Code signal that the Navigational Aid transmits. Once you have done so you can be sure you are heading the right way and you have to follow it. If the signal is not correct, you cannot trust it.

Just like Jesus said that "The sheep that are *My own hear and are listening to My voice*; and I know them, and *they follow Me*." in John 10:27, you must listen in for His voice and follow it. Do not listen to other voices, they are false signals and will lead you the wrong way.

Once you have verified you've got the right frequency and signal, you'll receive directions from the ATC to join the course inbound that will take you to your destination. The ATC will again be "vectoring" you precisely in order for you to join the course that will lead you in.

What you'll be looking at is this instrument inside the cockpit on your instrument panel. First of all, these instruments have a little triangle "flag" telling you if you are receiving a good signal from the station. Secondly, depending on what type of an approach you are planning on to your destination, the flag may also point the direction where the station is in reference to you.

The instrument will also have what we call a "needle" that will give you the course guidance to the left and right as needed to stay on course. Some instruments will also have another needle that will give you "Glide Slope" indications. Glide Slope needle will give you guidance to descend at the correct descend angle to the destination.

These needles are like the Holy Spirit. Just like the Holy Spirit should remain in the center of our lives, these needles should remain in the center of the instrument.

Once you have intercepted these "needles" that we call **CDI**'s, "**C**ourse **D**eviation **I**ndicators, all you have to do is to follow them. If any of the CDI needles deflect to the left or right, up or down, all you need is minor attitude adjustments to put them back to the center. If you don't make these small corrections to your attitude, the deviations will become greater and greater and eventually will take you off your course. The reason then for you not landing at your destination is not that the signal was not there and the direction was not given, but that you did not follow the guidance in front of you.

There's a limit how far you can be off course. When large enough deviations happen, for whatever reason, we need to go for "missed approach". What that means is that we abort the approach to that destination for the moment before things get totally out of hand and outright dangerous and follow the missed approach directions. The good news is that unless the outside circumstances were the reason for abandoning the approach - such like a bad weather - we get to try it again. The ATC will give us new "vectors", which are our new directions to follow in order to get us to re-intercept the course that will lead us in to our destination airport giving us another chance.

CHAPTER FOUR

Wisdom Nugget #4

You'll never forget when
you learn from your own
mistakes, but it is easier to
learn from others. It is
much less painful and it
is by far less expensive!

CHAPTER FOUR

Practical Jokes

www.chickenwingscomics.com

Every so often pilots are playing some practical jokes on each other as the opportunity arises. These can be great learning opportunities also for the one that the joke is played on.

In aviation there are what we call "practice areas" that are designated for concentrated flight training areas. These areas usually share a common frequency where we can announce our location to other traffic as a common courtesy so we can be more vigilant as to the particular locations where others are flying.

Sometimes a pilot supposing to have changed the frequency back to ATC wishing to request radar vectors back for an approach to an airfield forgets to actually change the frequency and is making the request on the practice area frequency. Just then someone else is pretending to be the ATC and responds to the pilot giving them totally wrong directions to fly based on their location, (as long as there is no chance of endangerment due to visibility and you are not being led in the blind, of course).

Unless the pilot recognizes something is wrong, he will be flying completely wrong direction. This usually does get the pilot's attention, however and then everyone laughs about it. Once the joke is over, hopefully the pilot will get smart and always double check the frequency he is listening and transmitting on.

Another thing about transmitting on the radio, you've always got to think about what you are saying. You could have a stuck microphone. This has happened more than once and I have listened to conversations that we should not have been hearing. Lesson learned, watch what you are saying. Someone else besides you may be listening to you.

The Traffic Controller is Looking Out for You

...That is if you got the right frequency and are listening to the authentic controller, of course. The real Controllers are there to direct you and help you. They are your resource and they are the ones with the view of other traffic and the weather surrounding you.

However, when you are flying an airplane, you are considered to be either the **PIC**, **P**ilot **I**n **C**ommand or the **SIC**, **S**econd **I**n **C**ommand of that airplane (if it requires a flight crew of two crew members to operate). What that means is that you have been given authority to *make the decisions* and *give the commands* to the airplane as to the direction it is supposed to be heading to and what kind of attitude it is flying since you have been given the controls of that aircraft. In other words, as a licensed pilot *you are putting forth the commands demanding the response* from that airplane and therefore you are really responsible for the outcome based on your *decisions*.

Now, you may listen to the ATC and consider the warnings or suggestions they might give you, or you can ignore them. It would behoove you, however, to consider their input and obey, but ultimately, you could decide against their directions since you have been given the license to fly that airplane and you are in it making the decisions as to where it is going.

The same way God has given us a free will of choice to do as we will. He much prefers that we willfully obey His leading and His direction. But, ultimately you must make that decision ourselves to trust, be willing and obedient to His call and know that He has your best in mind.

I was listening to a teaching of Kenneth Copeland about changing your way of thinking as he was sharing an experience he had one time flying his airplane. He was being directed away from his departure airport towards his destination when the Lord asked him why he wasn't upset for not having received his requested altitude. He had filed for 37,000 feet, but was flying at 11,000 feet.

He realized he had to change his way of thinking when he was asked this question by the Lord as it is quite natural for pilots not to receive a clearance to climb to your requested altitude from the very beginning. The Air Traffic Controller is looking at the radar and has a complete picture of everything around you and you are not the only one in the sky. As I mentioned before, it is an orchestrated sequence of many airplanes, weather and other factors in the same airspace sur-rounding you. Here you are in your little space called cockpit and that's all you can see. The ATC on the other hand sees everything about you and his job is to keep you clear of other traffic and weather as well.

As a pilot he knew well that it was only a matter of time and he would receive his requested altitude, but it wasn't going to be for some time. He knew that the ATC was doing their job of getting him out of their airspace safely and eventually, when the time was right he would get his clearance to climb to the requested altitude.

When he told the Lord that he knew he was going to get what he had asked for when the time was right, the Lord responded how He wished that all Christians would give Him the same respect and trust. Wow, what a revelation and so true.

God is the best Air Traffic Controller there is and He is not out to withhold from us anything. He is out there giving us directions so that we can reach our destinations on time and avoid pitfalls. After all, He can see the complete picture and the end from the beginning when we only see our own circumstances. Let's give Him the trust and respect He deserves. He has our best in mind.

Aeronautical Decision Making

ADM is **A**eronautical **D**ecision **M**aking and it refers to decisions that the pilots will have to make in everyday flying in different circumstances. Often it refers to unplanned situations that take place and a pilot is put in a position to meet a challenge that has risen un-announced.

This has become an even more important issue lately and the focus in training for pilots as the decisions that pilots make in these times could result in good outcomes or not so great. The solution is to give as many different scenarios as possible for the training pilot to consider and let them make their decisions based on their knowledge of all available information. It is impossible to cover every possible situation, but the more decisions you have had to make, the more prepared you will be to make the new ones as they appear.

The definition of **A**eronautical **D**ecision **M**aking is "a **systematic approach** to the mental process used by aircraft pilots to **consistently determine the best course of action** in response to a given set of circumstances". Can you imagine us as Christians using this approach in utilizing the Word of God, rightly dividing it and **consistently determining the best course of action in response to the devil** in *any* given circumstance?

The good news is that the devil has no new tricks! We can actually prepare ourselves to always have the right response to whatever it is that the enemy is trying to bring to us as a stumbling block. We can overcome it all by the Blood of the Lamb and the Word of our testimony. The Word has given us the tools to always be prepared to make the right decisions in every circumstance and to "read the devils mail" so to speak. As I said, he has no new tricks.

In **A**eronautical **D**ecision **M**aking, when situations so demand a pilot has the right to **take authority** given to him or her as a licensed pilot and make the right decisions to avert an undesirable outcome and a possible disaster. The same way as Christians, we have been given **authority to use Jesus' Name** to *command the devil to leave us* with his suggestions and deception, and *demand the promises given to us* in God's Word. This is our right given to us as our inheritance and as the children of the King.

CHAPTER FIVE

Wisdom Nugget #5

Whether you rise or fall is
based on your Attitude.
But, it is the source of
power that *keeps* you
in the air!

CHAPTER FIVE

More about Attitude

We had a discussion one day with a good friend of ours, Arch Bishop Roger Smyzer. He was sharing with us what God had revealed to him regarding the definition of sin. When he was sharing it I realized it totally related to this book I was writing and I had to ask him if I could share his revelation with everyone in this book. He agreed. To the best of my ability I will attempt to relay here what he shared.

He said, "sin can be defined as any *improper attitude* towards the activities of God, man or satan, as those activities interact in my life or in the lives of those around me. Improper activity then is me having a *selfish attitude* towards that circumstance." He continued, "All of our actions are supposed to be selfless. Jesus said 'I do not my own purpose. My judgment is always right'. The nature of that statement has everything to do with someone else. It shows *servant* **attitude**. In fact, when you look closely, the entire Bible can be capped in one word, **attitude**."

I never really looked at it this way, but everywhere you look in the Bible, there is an attitude or a result of an attitude displayed. The attitudes are either correct or improper attitudes towards something or someone.

The very next week after having this discussion with our friend, I was watching Keith Moore teaching in Kenneth Copeland's TV program about sin. Listening to his teaching I kept hearing the same underlining of **attitude** towards the activity or someone or a thing. For example, if you have a relaxed attitude about something that is not all that correct thing to do, but say to yourself, "everyone else is doing it", that improper **attitude** towards the thing or activity would be the sin. You can simply *change the* **attitude** and there would be no more sin concerning that. As an example, you have heard it said, "it is OK to look". But, the Bible says "he who even lusts after a woman has committed sin in their heart". So, your **attitude** about looking is improper, or wrong, towards that thing, person or activity. Therefore, the sin is the improper **attitude**.

Wow, an improper attitude in flight can kill you if left unrecognized and so can improper attitude in life! It can lead to short life and even death spiritually as it is a sin. It is critical then for us to recognize our improper attitudes if we are to correct any of them, just like it would be imperative in flight to recognize wrong attitudes. Otherwise you wouldn't correct the wrong attitude and as we all know by now, in flight it would be detrimental.

So, watch your attitude! Pay attention to it. Search your heart and examine what the Bible teaches us about everyday life. Then line up with the Wisdom you gain from the Word and you will live a clean life of a good attitude and reap the Blessings promised to you in the Bible.

Your Attitude Determines Your Altitude

Your attitude does determine your altitude, but there's another element that's also needed, and that's power. You must put some power behind your attitude in order to climb to new horizons! This power scripturally is your words.

Just like the airplane needs fuel to be powered up, so do we as Christians need to put the Word of God into our mouths. That's the fuel to raise us up to higher levels. Unless you are a glider and don't have an engine, you need to put the fuel into the tank. If you are a glider, that means you must be a new Christian, or not yet developed in the Word since you are relying on outside source to provide you the lift. You cannot forever rely on *other* people bailing you out and your pastor praying on your behalf every time if you are not doing anything to improve yourself and take authority over your own situation. Eventually you must develop yourself in the Word of God and get you some engines of your own with a fuel tank in order to become what God envisioned you to be.

You also need to put the *right* fuel into the tank so your engine can run. The wrong fuel will kill the engine and gets you down real fast. The same way, the wrong words will also pull you down really fast. That could drastically adjust your attitude the wrong way and make it a very bad day for you - as well as others!

Not only should you put good fuel into your engines, but you can also upgrade your engines into more powerful ones. You can build your spirit up by studying and meditating on God's Word continuously and therefore become a powerhouse for God! It's like changing your airplane into a new one with more powerful engines. Eventually you'll be upgrading to a jet that can propel you to higher altitudes and fly faster to your destination and to the dream which God placed in your heart.

High Altitude Flying

Once you upgrade to a jet, you'll be flying higher than ever before. Jets are designed to fly high. High altitude flying is considered to take place when you are flying at altitudes in excess of 25,000 feet. There is special training involved if you are to do high altitude flying. As you can imagine, the pressure around you changes as you climb to higher. There is less oxygen at higher altitudes and the air gets less dense around you. As the air thins, you are not only moving faster through the air, but the pressure differential between the atmosphere inside the airplane and the outside is also getting larger. Therefore, you need some extra help flying out there and you need to go through some extra training to understand the possible hazards involved with high altitude flying and how to operate when flying high.

One thing that is crucial is a pressurized aircraft. Unless you are inside a pressurized vessel, you are not protected from the harmful elements of high altitude. The pressure differential alone is enough to make a difference between life and death.

Think about a balloon that is filled with helium. Now imagine that same balloon lifting through the atmosphere. As it climbs higher and higher, guess what happens to the helium inside the balloon. It expands! As the air inside the balloon keeps expanding, the balloon keeps growing, until the skin of the balloon just gives up and all the air escapes as the balloon breaks.

That would basically be the case for us as well when it comes to the air in our lungs. As the air would expand, so would the air in our lungs expand and find its way out. This is especially true in the case of a "rapid decompression", which is a sudden depressurization of an aircraft. When the pressure differential between the inside of the airplane and the air outside goes away, the air is suddenly sucked out of our lungs and "*decompression sickness*" could result. Decompression sickness is a physiological disorder caused by a rapid decrease in atmospheric pressure, which results in the release of nitrogen bubbles into body tissues. In other words, those bubbles are like gas balloons inside body tissue and joints and along with altitude they expand, therefore causing pain, nausea, even paralysis and death.

This decompression sickness could also result simply by not following the rules that one should not fly at altitudes above 8000 FT within 24 hours of scuba diving. This has to do with the nitrogen gases inside the body tissues that will take some time to release from the body as it gets used to the normal atmospheric pressure on earth after diving. The pressure increases as we go deeper down while diving just like it decreases as we go higher. So, the lower you have let the devil push you in your life, the more pressure you have allowed yourself to be exposed to. Come back above the water and once you have adjusted, let's fly higher with God than you've ever been!

Normally if you are flying inside a pressurized vessel -like an airplane with a pressurization system- the cabin will not climb at the same rate as the surrounding space. Therefore your body has the chance to adjust as the atmosphere does not change at such a rapid rate and besides slowing down the decreasing pressure inside the cabin, the system also does not allow it to go beyond the comfortable levels.

I think of the pressurized vessel like the airplane as the protective shield of the Spirit, the Faith and the Anointing, which keeps us safe from the deathly elements of the cruel world surrounding us. Depressurization then would be deflation of the Spirit, Faith and the Anointing. So, to remain protected, you must stay in the Word and in the Spirit. Keep the Anointed and His Anointing in your life. Spend time in the Word and fill your spirit with His Spirit daily, in other words, keep yourself "pressurized" and protected from the outer darkness.

Aeromedical Factors Related to High Altitude Flying

If you are not protected from the atmospheric conditions of the high altitude, there are some other symptoms besides decompression sickness that you could encounter. Here are few examples:

Hypoxia. This is lack of oxygen in the body. The symptoms can include *deteriorating vision (limited, blurred, tunnel vision), sleepiness, dizziness, headache, euphoria, impaired judgment and confusion, incapacitation* and *unconsciousness* to mention a few.

Spiritual Hypoxia would be the lack of Word in your life. If you lack the life giving Word, you could encounter some of the symptoms such as *lack of vision for your life* and feeling *tired* along with lack of motivation, making wrong decisions in your life, in other words, *having the lack of judgment.* You are probably *not feeling so great physically* either and still, possibly you may be in the state of *"euphoria"* thinking that all is OK, that's the way life is.

Perhaps you are feeling a little *confused* about what you are supposed to be doing here on earth and are feeling inadequate (*incapacitated*). Maybe you do not even recognize anything is missing! That would be a totally *unconscious* state. The way to fix the Hypoxic state is, of course get some oxygen in you. Go to the Word and put on the Word Oxygen Mask!

Hyperventilation is a totally opposite of Hypoxia as this occurs when an individual is experiencing emotional stress, fright, or pain, and the breathing rate and depth increase, although the carbon dioxide level in the blood is already at a reduced level. The result is an excessive loss of carbon dioxide from the body, which can lead to unconsciousness. So, there is an imbalance of the required elements in your body. Corrective action is to slow down breathing to increase CO_2 by *talking aloud* or breathing into a paper bag.

So, if you encounter supernatural hyperventilation, TALK OUT LOUD! Supernatural hyperventilation happens when you are *not* full of the Word of God and you consider the doubts that the enemy puts in your head. You experience emotional stress, fright, or pain, just like during hyperventilation. Stop those thoughts by talking the Word OUT LOUD! Remember, you cannot continue thinking the enemy's thoughts when you talk out loud the Word of God.

You've got to simply doubt the devils doubts, like I heard Jesse Duplantis, a great minister from Louisiana say during one of his sermons. It is so true. How do you doubt the devils doubts? By KNOWING what God has said and taking Him at His Word. By rehearsing continuously what He has promised. By believing God when He said that …

He will watch over His Word to perform it in Jeremiah 1:12

…and that **His Word shall not return to Him void in Isaiah 55:11**.

It is impossible for God to lie. - Hebrews 6:18

CHAPTER SIX

Wisdom Nugget #6

When you trust
in God's Word,
Satan's illusions
won't make a lick
of difference.

CHAPTER SIX

Disorientation

Unless you trust your instruments, it would be very easy to become disoriented when flying without the outside reference and feeling the outside forces affecting the airplane. Kinesthetic sense is very unreliable, because the body can't tell the difference between gravity and G-loads. Visual illusions (especially at night) can make it worse. We have touched this subject earlier when talking about trusting your instruments, i.e. trusting the Word. Don't be fooled by the devil's illusions and symptoms. Don't go by sense feelings, believe the Word only.

In aviation, vestibular disorientation comes from forces on the hair cells of the three semicircular canals in your inner ear. These illusions are:

Coriolis illusion - moving the head quickly creates an illusion of rotating or turning. While this is not really even happening, it certainly feels like it is, because our body's sensing system. This involves the simultaneous stimulation of two semicircular canals in *the inner ear*. Do not let the devil mess with your inner ear by letting him send wrong messages there trying to deceive you!

Since this illusion is associated with a sudden tilting (forward or backwards) of the pilot's head while the aircraft is turning, it can occur when you tilt your head down, for example to look at an approach chart or to write a note on your knee pad, or tilt it up - to look at an overhead instrument or switch - or tilt it sideways. This produces an almost unbearable sensation that the aircraft is rolling, pitching up or down, and yawing left or right all at the same time, which can be compared with the sensation of rolling down on a hillside. This illusion can make the pilot quickly become disoriented and lose control of the aircraft.

So if you let the devil influence where you look he has access to your senses and can mess with your head. If a pilot does not pay attention to the instruments, you can see that he or she could put the aircraft into a totally wrong attitude only because they made an input based on the feeling without taking the time to interpret what really is happening. Therefore, it is crucial you stay focused on the Word only.

If you do not totally rely on God and His Word as the only truth you, too, could respond incorrectly based on the world's input to your sensory systems.

Somatogravic illusion - when acceleration feels like nose-high attitude and deceleration feels like a dive. These feelings have to do with the G-forces and again, are illusions.

The first one is **the head-up illusion.** It involves a sudden forward linear acceleration during level flight where the pilot perceives the illusion that the nose of the aircraft is pitching up. The pilot's response to this illusion would be to push the yoke (the control column, which is the "steering wheel" of the airplane in the air) forward to pitch the nose of the aircraft down. A night take-off from a well-lit airport into a totally dark sky or a catapult take-off from an aircraft carrier can also lead to this illusion, and could result in a crash.

The head-down illusion involves a sudden linear deceleration (air breaking by lowering of flaps, decreasing engine power) during level flight where the pilot perceives the illusion that the nose of the aircraft is pitching down. The pilot's response to this illusion would be to raise the nose of the aircraft up. If this illusion occurs during a low-speed final approach, the pilot could stall the aircraft.

If you keep your eyes on the instruments you will not be interpreting incorrectly what you should be doing and therefore you will keep your airplane flying straight and level. So, keep on the straight and narrow path and do not be moved by the devil's suggestions.

Inversion illusion - change from climb to level feels like tumbling backward. Inversion illusions may occur when gravity reference signals are gone, just like when changing from climb attitude to a level flight and there is a moment of weightlessness.

Perhaps you are constantly changing your attitude suddenly. This could possibly make you feel like you are tumbling backwards. So, what's the solution to avoid this? Keep more even attitude and change your course only by the reference to your instruments. In other words, rely on the Word and the leading of the Holy Spirit. Don't react to the world.

Graveyard spiral - prolonged constant-rate turn may be interpreted as wings-level descent. Eventually, this will lead into ever steepening spiral downwards while all along we think all is well. If we do not listen to the increasing noise created by the increasing airspeed as the plane accelerates downward towards the earth and neither do pay attention to the signs given by the instruments, graveyard spiral will end up to a certain death.

Leans - recovery to a bank (in a tilted position) is interpreted by inner ear as a roll in the opposite direction. If we feel we are leaning into one direction, but indeed are flying straight and level, we may attempt to "correct" the flight attitude based on our feelings and turn the opposite direction. A false sensation of banking (sense of a turn in one direction) can occur when pilots direct their gaze away from the instrument display. So, too, if we walk by feelings and do not keep our eyes on the Word, we may turn in the wrong direction.

Others - autokinesis, false horizons, haze, empty field myopia.

Two illusions that lead to spatial disorientation, the **false horizon** and **autokinesis**, are concerned with the visual system. *In the dark*, a stationary light will *ap-*

pear to move about when stared at for many seconds. The disoriented pilot could lose control of the aircraft in attempting to align it with the false movements of this light. This is called **autokinesis**. Even the enemy can come as a false light. You know he cannot lead you anywhere good and too much attention to that light will align you on a wrong path. Make sure that the light you are looking at lines up with the Word of God.

A sloping cloud formation, an obscured horizon, an aurora borealis, a dark scene spread with ground lights and stars, and certain geometric patterns of ground lights can provide inaccurate visual information, or **false horizon**, for aligning the aircraft correctly with the actual horizon. The disoriented pilot may place the aircraft in a dangerous attitude.

The same way, if you are trying to follow some worldly example or advise that does not line up with the Word of God, it is definitely not for your good and can even lead to destruction of God's plan for your life. Instead, be attentive to hear God's direction for your life and do not try to align yourself with the world.

Haze and **fog** can be a particularly dangerous. Penetration of fog can create an illusion of pitching up. Pilots who do not recognize this illusion will often steepen the approach for landing quite abruptly.

The absence of any detail in clear blue sky, fog or haze makes it difficult for eyes to focus on infinity. When there's no detail, the focus of the eye constantly changes! This is called **empty field myopia** and could be recognized also in our daily lives if we lack focus.

So, there are two things we need to be aware of. First, there are illusions created by the enemy that he would rather have us focus on than pay attention to the Word of God. These are simply distractions (**F**alse **E**vidences **A**ppearing **R**eal) that he throws at us to get us away from trusting the Word. If he cannot get us to receive his suggestions, he then tries to take our attention away from the Word all together. This way he could get us into the empty field of myopia where we won't see anything. In other words, he is trying to blind us from seeing God's plan for our lives. He is constantly trying to change our focus to a point that we won't follow through with anything and therefore will not be faithful stewards of what God has called us to do and attend to.

Do you know what FOCUS consists of? It means **F**ollow **O**ne **C**ourse **U**ntil **S**uccessful! If you stay in the Word and follow that one course until you hear from the Lord yourself where and what direction He is leading you on, you will be successful, because you will KNOW you are in the midst of His Will for your life.

So what's the answer to all of these illusions? Check, and believe, your instruments. Do not go by your feelings. Only trust and believe the Word.

F.O.C.U.S

I want to talk a bit more about **F**ollow **O**ne **C**ourse **U**ntil **S**uccessful. It is kind of like taking one step at a time or eating one bite at a time. This is exactly what you would do with any kind of learning or moving towards any goal and destination you may have.

Mary Kay Ash, the founder of Mary Kay Cosmetics once asked "how do you eat an elephant"? (Not that you would want to). But, for illustration purposes only, you wouldn't want to even try eating an elephant all in one bite. You couldn't. So how would you do it? You would eat one bite at a time, of course. Just the same way you will learn new skills and the same way you will follow the leading of the Lord, one step at a time.

This works the same way in flight training. I heard a great true story from Kenneth Copeland, who is a minister of the Gospel as well as a pilot. When he was learning to fly many years ago, he couldn't wait to finally fly solo in the airplane he had been flying with the instructor along with him all this time. Then came the day he was allowed to "fly out of the nest" so to speak and to take the plane up by himself for the first time.

Up to this point, he had been flying early in the morning when it was calm and barely any other traffic around, but his solo flight took place at 4 pm in the afternoon. This meant that in Dallas Fort Worth area where he was getting his training, there was some airline traffic around at this time also and he was not alone in the air.

So, routinely he takes off and makes his turn to join downwind position preparing for another left turn for left base and then to final, just like he always has in the past. He reports his position to the control tower and the tower to his amazement comes up with a long line of instructions all at once and tells him he is number 8 in line to the field and that he is to "follow the DC9 over the outer marker". At this point, he has no clue as to what was said and so he reports, "sir, this is my first solo…" to which the tower responds, "no problem. Just continue on that heading and altitude. I will tell you when to make your turn". This made it a whole lot more simple, one step at a time.

So, when God gives us directions, He may not show us the whole picture all at once. We may not be ready for it yet and may choke at the directions if it came to us all at once or too early in our training. He knows to feed us spoon by spoon. As we grow up and develop in the Word we are able to take in a lot more information and digest a lot more than just milk. But, there is always timing for everything and you can't rush things to make them happen faster than you are ready. God knows the timing for everything and everyone much better than we do. So, trust him. He will let you know when you are ready for the next step. But, it is up to us to show ourselves approved.

2 Tim 2:15 Study to shew thyself approved unto God, a workman that needeth not to be ashamed, rightly dividing the word of truth (KJV).

Even in flight training, there are steps to reach the next level and there is always an instructor who will determine if the student is ready to take the flight test. Before that day arrives, the instructor is not going to sign the student off to move on to the next step. It takes more than just instruction to get a pilot license. It takes preparation also on the student's part and willingness to learn. Besides that, there are minimum requirements to fulfill.

A good student will work diligently at everything needed with the goal in mind to pass the final test and graduate. If the student follows the directions of the instructor and follows the guide lines set for the test, he or she will pass the test. Much the same way God is watching us to see if we are doing our due diligence preparing the way for our next step up. But, sometimes we are just not doing our part and there's nothing else God can do to move us higher.

You have probably heard the saying that "you can lead the horse to the water, but you cannot make him to drink. The same way a pastor can lead you to the Light of the Word or a flight instructor can teach the best he knows how, but if you are not willing to learn you will not receive the blessing. That's the same way God and the Holy Spirit works. He is a gentleman. He is not going to push His way, but it would be to our benefit to stay connected to the vine, just like Jesus told us in John 15. After all, He is our source of life and everything good and pleasant.

Most of us want to grow and receive from the Lord all that He has for us. But, if everything seems to be staying the same old same old in our lives, most likely it's not us waiting on the Lord. It's really Him waiting on us. Also, when the scripture says to "wait on the Lord" in Psalm 37:34, it does not refer to us just sitting and stagnating. It refers to us waiting on, like serving the Lord, to eagerly wait for, expect and look unto Him.

Ps. 37:34 Wait on the LORD, and keep his way, and he shall exalt thee to inherit the land: when the wicked are cut off, thou shalt see it.

So, instead of having Him eagerly waiting on us, let us eagerly expect and look unto Him, serving the Lord.

Short time ago, the Lord showed me in Luke 19:26 in Amplified Bible how it says (in Newman translation) "if you *get* and have, more will be given to you and if you don't, even that which you have will be taken from you!"

Luke 19:26 And [said Jesus,] I tell you that to everyone who gets *and* has will more be given, but

from the man who does not get *and* does not have, even what he has will be taken away.

Another confirmation of this is in Deuteronomy 8:18.

Deut 8:18 But you shall [earnestly] remember the Lord your God, for it is He Who gives you power to get wealth, that He may establish His covenant which He swore to your fathers, as it is this day.

He emphasized how the word **get** is an action word. How many times do you see someone who wants to have more in life, but they are just too lazy to go **get** it? They simply want a hand out and remain stagnant, never achieving their full potential. Maybe you even recognize this in you! If you do, I hope to awaken you from your sleep to **go get** what your heart's desire is and go to work on it! The graveyard is already full of buried dreams, songs not composed and books not written. Don't let it be you. God gave all of us full potential to accomplish His purpose in life. He is faithful to reveal His will for your life if you only show yourself approved, be diligent and **F**ollow **O**ne **C**ourse **U**ntil **S**uccessful.

Levels of Learning

So God feeds us spoon by spoon and leads us step by

step. We are getting our vision a piece at a time so we are not choking at the information coming at us. Until God develops our vision inside, and we grow our faith to stretch with His, we could not contain His vision for us. God thinks only BIG and we need to learn to do the same.

Just like in any learning, in aviation there are four levels of learning. These are Rote, Understanding, Applying and Correlating. Let's briefly study each level and see how this corresponds with us studying the Word of God as we gain more deep understanding of it.

First, there is the **Rote** level. Rote simply means to *repeat* or *copy*. It does not mean you understand the thing, but you are simply repeating what the teacher says. You are quoting the Word, perhaps repeating after the pastor, or reading the Word out loud. This level of learning is fairly prevalent in aviation studying during the initial training while preparing for the written portion of the exam. Often student rehearses the same questions and answers in preparation that eventually he or she may simply remember the answer, but really does not yet have the foundation to understand the underlying causes of the subject. Eventually, the student must progress to the next level, which is *understanding*.

Understanding then is the *revelation* of the subject matter. Understanding is knowing why something works the way it does, why do the wings fly, why does the plane accelerate and climb when you add power etc.

In aviation, it's understanding the aerodynamics of why an airplane flies and therefore gaining confidence in its power to uphold you and keep you in the air. This same happens when you begin to understand what you are repeating after the pastor or reading in God's Word and the revelation comes to you. All of the sudden, you are gaining confidence in God's Word and its power to do what it was sent to do. This is when you get really happy and know that you are making progress. Now that you understand a thing, the very next step is, of course, to apply it.

Application of the revelation is to put it to use. Now you are going to practice what you came to understand. You will rehearse it, because now you know *how* you are to use your new found knowledge. In aviation, you will learn what each control of the airplane does and then you go make it happen. You go practice. Now you know how it works. But, once you know how something works, you need to go to the next level and find where and *when* to put it to work. This part is the final level to complete the learning process and is called correlating.

Correlation is knowing in what circumstances something is to be used. For example, when we teach students to recover from unusual attitudes, the key element is knowing when to add power and when to take away power from the engines. In other words, if you are in a nose dive, the last thing you should ever do is to add power to your engines. That move will just accelerate your descend to the earth! On the other hand, if you are about to stall the airplane and your airspeed is slowing down, you'd better add some power to your engines to help the airplane maintain its altitude and airspeed.

Correlation then becomes essential to learning in anything if you were to fully take advantage of the knowledge. Otherwise, you are plain dangerous with partial information and could wrongfully use it. Dr. Myles Monroe from Bahamas Faith Ministries once said "if you do not know the purpose of the thing you will abuse it". This is so true.

When reading God's Word, you'll find yourself at different stages at different times. The more you spend time in His Word, the deeper understanding and the deeper level you will get in His Word. Eventually, you'll start seeing correlations in His Word and in your life's situations. That's when you have reached the highest level for that particular element in your live and that is never ending. There is a continuous revelation in God's Word.

I have found that the more you meditate in God's Word in conjunction with your passion, whatever that is, the more connection and correlation you'll start seeing between the Word and what you love. So, keep reading, studying and meditating upon the Word of God and thinking on the things nearest to your heart. Find your passion and keep meditating on the end result. After all, God is the one that has put that dream in your heart. Soon you'll start getting revelation from Gods Word and direction in which to go to fulfill your purpose.

It really is like building blocks that come together and eventually form a building, or pieces of a puzzle that in the end complete a beautiful picture.

God is the Master Builder and we were all put on this earth to finish His plan and creation, to complete His Vision, of which we are such an integral part. Make it a fun journey of continuous revelation!

CHAPTER SEVEN

Wisdom Nugget # 7

Don't just wait for
Avalanche, be part of it!
Sow your snow on the
mountain.

CHAPTER SEVEN

Avalanche

Talking about the revelations, let's take a little side trip from Aviation related revelations to talk about another parallel from nature. I will tie this overall subject into aviation at the end of this chapter.

So many revelations I have received from the Lord has been inspired by the teaching we receive at the Words of Life Fellowship Church in North Miami. It takes only one Word from God that can change your life, if you hear the *Voice behind* the Word. One of these is the word Avalanche that was released during one Sunday service. The word just exploded inside of me as it did in many other members of the congregation. It kept growing in me as the Lord would reveal things relating to this word.

This wasn't just any ordinary word, but it was becoming a parable of what was really going on from the Spiritual to the natural world. You see, when I was meditating on this word, I started seeing a picture of how Avalanche would become into fullness. As the Lord was speaking to me about it I started to write what I saw.

When you are sowing you are "snowing" your snow-flakes on top of your mountain of Blessing and build-ing an Avalanche! Each flake of different and indi-vidual design is your seed. Be they acts of kindness, financial seed or any other, together they will build up to a weighty load of Glory on top of the mountain, until one day it will not be able to hold it and it must release it. Then it will release the Avalanche of Bless-ings that overtake you!

There are many Mountains of Blessings also, many ministries, many ways to sow your snow and when you sow many ways it will come on you many ways and from all directions. Weather you lay your seed di-rectly on top of the mountain or sow it into the lives of the least fortunate, God will always create out of it the most beautiful snow flake and it will be found on top of the mountain and be part of your Avalanche of Blessings.

Just like a cloud will release one snow flake at a time and they descend on top of the mountain until the load becomes so heavy that the mountain cannot contain it any longer. All it takes is a little noise or one more snow flake and the mountain will have to release it and it becomes an avalanche. The same way I saw we must sow our seeds to release our Avalanche of Blessings into our lives.

So our giving is like snowflakes, big and small, each flake of individual design descending on top of the mountain until it becomes so heavy it becomes an avalanche. It is like God's Glory (Glory meaning Heavy, Weighty) descending on us like an avalanche. The mountain then is God's throne, or an altar, where we lay our gifts. When you are sowing, you are "snowing" your snowflakes on top of your Mountain of Blessing and building an avalanche.

What if there was no snow given by the cloud? Then there would be no avalanche. What if there was no seed sown? Then there can't be any harvest, no blessing overtaking us. So then, this is like a continuous Life Cycle, one thing feeding and triggering another. Your next seed may just be that one more snow flake on top of the mountain that will release your avalanche. The faster we load the faster we release it into our lives.

Once I saw this, the Lord clearly said, "Don't just wait for Avalanche, be part of it! Sow your snow on the mountain." Whatever you do, do not stop placing the flakes on top of the mountain! Be a BLESSING!

Voice Behind the Word

Let's dig deeper into the *Voice behind* the word. This is really what the revelation is all about. You could be listening to a sermon or reading the Word or a book and in the midst of it you get a revelation. What's happening is really you are hearing the Voice behind the Word or the sermon and God is now getting through to *you*.

Remember, that Jesus is the Word of God. But, who and what is Jesus to you? The most correct answer really is *He is whatever you need Him to be to you right now.* He is everything we need! He is the Word of God, The Word that heals, The Word that supplies all of our needs, The Word that protects, The light shining on our path leading us where we should go. He is The Ever Present Help in time of need.

The Amplified Bible says in Johns Gospel,

If you live in Me [abide vitally united to Me] and My <u>words</u> remain in you and continue to live in your hearts, ask <u>whatever</u> you will, and it shall be done for you. - John 15:7. (AMP)

The Word is alive and is the **substance** of everything we need.

Did you also know that the word for *"word"* and *"thing"* have the same meaning in Greek? They are the *same thing*! So, if the Word and the thing is the same thing, then all things are already provided to us in His Word! Whatsoever **things** you ask for according to His **Word** you shall receive. Your hearts desires will manifest.

Delight yourself also in the Lord, and He will give you the desires and secret petitions of your heart. Commit your way to the Lord [roll and repose each care of your load on Him]; trust (lean on, rely on, and be confident) also in Him and He will bring it to pass. - Ps. 37: 4-5 (AMP)

You know the Word also says, **"<u>*Faith*</u> is the <u>*substance*</u> of things hoped for and the <u>*evidence*</u> of *things* not (yet) seen." in Hebrews 11:1.**

So notice, that first of all it is **Faith** that is the **substance** and the **evidence**.

Secondly, the Word says that "*Faith* comes by *hearing* and *hearing* by the Word of God." - **Romans 10:17.**

Amplified Bible says it like this **"So faith comes by hearing [what is told]** (or preached)**, and what is heard comes by the preaching [of the message that <u>came from the lips</u>] of Christ (the Messiah Himself)."** Let me expound on that.

First Hope arises when you read or listen to His Word. This hope gives you light and enlightenment until it enables your understanding to hear His Voice. When that happens, you get the revelation and your faith builds up until the Word is just more real to you than this world.

So then **Faith** (the substance and the evidence) comes when you hear the **Voice**, the **Revelation behind the Word** that you read or listen to continuously. In Newman translation Romans 10:17 says that, "*Faith* comes by *hearing* and *hearing by the Voice*, the *Revelation* of and through the Word of God."

So in conclusion, Faith is the substance and the evidence of the things you are hoping for, believing God for. Faith comes to us by hearing the Word of God, paying attention to it, putting it into our ears and our eyes and getting it into our hearts. It then gives us light end enlightenment through His Holy Spirit, who is our teacher, who helps us understand His Word until we hear His Voice behind the Word and receive revelation of it. Revelation then will bring us Faith and Faith is the substance we need in our everyday lives.

Now, how will you tune into the right frequency and hear His Voice behind the Word? By attending to His Word, of course.

God has given us our own radio that we need to tune in to receive His transmissions. The radio equipment is the Bible, our understanding is the receiver and the Holy Spirit is the frequency. Tune in your receiver to hear His transmissions to you by attending to His Word.

Weather Related

Weather report: Vertical visibility zero.

Pilot : "Is that in feet or meters?"

As I was pondering on the word Avalanche, the Lord started revealing to me other things relating to the subject. This is relating to the life cycle of the natural things and how everything naturally continues flowing in life.

The Lord pointed out how the rain falls from the sky and waters the earth and makes the seed grow on the earth and brings out the harvest. If there was no rain there would be no increase and the earth would dry up. As the Lord was speaking I started writing as fast as I could. The following is what I wrote:

[Sowing and reaping, seed time and harvest, so is the continuous life cycle of nature. The rain falls down from heaven and waters the earth. The earth gives moisture back into the atmosphere. It rises back up, forms the clouds of rain and more rain fills the earth and produces life. So it is continuous cycle.

If the earth kept all the rain it would flood and choke the seed. Then there would no longer be rain to water the seed in season as the clouds would not form to give the rain. Eventually the earth would become barren, void of everything, void of every living thing. Therefore, it is the cycle of life.

The same way is the seed that I provide. It is for you to release back and sow, so it can produce in your life the harvest, the avalanche of Blessings. Then you'll have more to sow and so it continues.]

Then He gave me the revelation of the things relating to this life cycle.

The earth is what you already have (your possessions). Some of it is a seed. God gives the rain (your tithe and some more seed to sow). Rain is also the Blessing that is the catalyst for all things to prosper in your hand. But, unless you release some of it, you'll choke your seed and rot your harvest as you'd hoard the rain & flood your storehouses. It is meant to keep flowing and moving to give room for more.

Rules and Regulations

So we know there are laws, like the law of gravity and the law of lift, the law of seed time and harvest. There are rules and regulations to abide by. There are also consequences for not following them. But we also know there are rewards for being obedient.

Let's say that you wanted to fly from Miami to New York. Instead of following the directions from ATC you didn't pay any attention to them and disregarded the regulations pertaining to your flight, do you think the authorities would just shrug their shoulders and say, "I guess he wants to go his own way, he must know better than us"? Of course not. Not only would you not reach your destination as you would possibly be intercepted by military, but for not following the rules you would also be in a heap of trouble. You probably would lose your privilege to fly and end up in front of a judge trying to defend yourself. This is kind of what happens when you want to do what *you* want to do and you make up your own rules to get what *you* want in life disregarding others. This would be selfishness.

On the other hand, if you flew by the rules and to the best of your ability obeyed every direction and instruction given by the ATC, you will land at your destination safely and as timely as possible.

What I appreciate and respect about my husband the most is the fact that when he gets directions from the Lord in his personal life, he will not deviate from it once he is clear and committed to something. He will stick to the vow he makes and the instruction he receives from the Lord. No wavering or questioning about it.

This is exactly what we are instructed to do in our lives in Ecclesiastes.

When you vow a vow or make a pledge to God, do not put off paying it; for God has no pleasure in

fools (those who witlessly mock Him). Pay what you vow. - Eccl. 5:4 (AMP)

So when God instructs us to do something and we pledge to comply, we must do it. That's what it says in the Word and we must obey it.

How about when we want to receive something from God? What do the rules say then?

James 1:6 in Amplified Bible says, **Only it must be in faith that he asks with no wavering (no hesitating, no doubting). For the one who wavers (hesitates, doubts) is like the billowing surge out at sea that is blown hither and thither and tossed by the wind.**

So, the same rule applies, we should always be not wavering once you commit to something.

This is especially true in aviation during a situation like engine out in flight. In a multi-engine airplane you may have more choices, but if you only have one engine and that has just "left you", you've got to know the "ABC's".

What the ABC's stand for is the following: A for the Airspeed. You must trim the plane to fly the airspeed that we call the Best Glide. This Best Glide airspeed also means that you trim the airplane for the right **attitude**, which in turn gives you the best glide range and buys the most time for you to deal with the emergency. B is the Best field. You must turn to the best option available at the time. C is the checklist and communication to declare emergency, i.e. to ask for help and whatever resources you may need.

Whatever you do you always *first* fly the airplane and trim it for the best airspeed. Once you have selected the best field, you must **stick with your decision without wavering** and head on that way as the lower you descend the less of the options you'll have left. So, for the most successful outcome, pick the best option available and stick with it!

CHAPTER EIGHT

Wisdom Nugget #8

Look at the ants and see. It
is not your greatness that
makes the difference,
but your diligence.

CHAPTER EIGHT

False Evidences Appearing Real

Earlier we talked about disorientation and false horizons that could be detrimental to flight. This same can be disastrous to your life, if you believe the false evidences of the enemy. Of course, I am talking about fear (False Evidences Appearing Real).

Just last night I saw a dream that didn't make much sense, but I can tell that it is directly related to what I am writing about. Often times the Lord can really talk to you in a dream as they seem so real and you have your feelings and emotions involved in the dream. The Lord can really get your attention then as emotions are a powerful thing and they can make a strong impression.

I remember thinking in the dream that this feels like a bad dream, but it was so real I didn't think it was one. Basically, at one point I was a confident and successful business owner speaking in some sort of conference. The next moment I was going on an elevator with a friend of mine, who is a pilot and very ambitious as well in business world. Her sister was also along for the ride. We were supposed to go to the penthouse suite and as the elevator button was pressed, we went up so fast that it frightened me. At the same time I realized I had left my jacket and purse downstairs and when we pressed to stop the elevator on a floor as it was passing through 55th floor, we stopped somewhere around floor 58. I got out from the elevator thinking I didn't want to go further up, but was going to take another elevator down. I was still fearful of that fast up moving elevator.

After this, I never found an elevator to get me down and I wondered off from even the elevator that took me up to this point in search for one. All I was thinking was how could I have left my purple jacket and my purse downstairs and how come there are no other elevators in this building that I can find.

As I woke up from this dream I realized that there were so many parallels to what I have been writing.

First there was the element of confident and successful business person. I certainly felt that whatsoever I had set my hands to prospered and I was even fairly good at it. But, when it came to the fast climb in the elevator, the fear gripped me. I was not ready for that. This relates to what we talked about in the chapter for **F.O.C.U.S.** **F**ollow **O**ne **C**ourse **U**ntil **S**uccessful. Prepare to be ready and study the Word, learn about your calling and about His plan for your life. Again, here's the scripture to back this up:

2 Tim 2:15 Study to shew thyself approved unto God, a workman that needeth not to be ashamed, rightly dividing the word of truth (KJV).

I sense the fast ride in the elevator as being the plan of God for us and once we step in on His plan it was going to shoot us up very high so fast, so suddenly, we just needed to be ready for it. In that dream the fear was holding me back. The fear caused me to stop on a floor in between.

Why was I so fearful in that dream? I realized I had left my purple jacket and my purse downstairs. Perhaps that purple jacket represented my mantle from the Lord and I wasn't wearing it. I also left behind my purse which represented finances. I still feel I am to finance the Gospel and the mantle and the purse belonged together. As a matter of fact, I believe that there is only One Source, but many channels that God is going to use to fund and further the Gospel. One of the channels I do believe is this book. He inspired me to write it in order to use funds it produces for Him.

Another element was that once I stepped out from God's elevator (because of the fear I felt) I was lost wondering in search for my mantle and my purse. It was like I was wondering around in the wilderness. I realize with God there is no looking back. Just don't forget your mantle behind!

So, whatever your calling is, follow it fearlessly. All the rest will come to pass as the foundation is in place. And how do you find your calling? Study the Word and follow the leading in your heart, which is the peace.

I learned long ago from several teachings that we are to follow love and peace. One teaching was by Kenneth E. Hagin and another by Keith Moore. If you follow love and peace, you know you are led by God.

Particularly, in one teaching from Keith Moore, I recall learning that whatever decisions you need to make, stay still and follow the peace in your heart.

Sometimes it may not make sense with your head, but you have peace. Then you must follow it. I had then started to use this in my own life and there are several instances where there was no way of me knowing the outcome of things. But, should I have made the decision based on head knowledge or what made sense at the time, I would have been worse off later.

The key is to talk to the Lord just like He was there next to you, like a spouse or a friend whom you know so well that you do not need to *hear* the answer, but you *know* the answer when you ask. That's because you have peace when you ponder the right answer.

When you know someone well enough, you can sense whether they approve a thing or not. They do not need to say a word, but you know. That's the leading of the Holy Spirit. All you need to do is listen to the still small voice in your heart.

This goes back into tuning into the right frequency and learning the "radio talk". There is a special language we call "Aviation Lingo" that pilots learn to talk. We consider that the standard radio phraseology so when everyone talks the same language we can all understand each other. The same way when you tune in with God you learn His language, His way of thinking and you can both understand each other. And then, of course, there is the Heavenly language that only God and you can communicate together with and the outsider like the devil is left out of that conversation.

The Ten Talents

Several years ago, when I was a brand new Christian, I was reading the story about the ten talents in **Matthew 25:14-30**. Then the Lord asked me, "which one of these servants are you going to be?" It wasn't an audible voice, but a very clear voice inside of me and very alive and real.

Of course, I answered I was going to be the one with ten talents. I have never forgotten it. It is like God Himself is continually reminding me of the promise I made to Him then and it has never left me. Any time that I have either run a business or done anything, I am reminded to be that profitable servant with all the talents that He had given to me, to give whatever I was doing a 100% and more.

Over the years He has added to that revelation the fact that we are to go and *get* wealth (to *get* profit) with the talents we have been given. We talked more about that also in the chapter called **F.O.C.U.S.**, where I shared those scriptures from **Luke 19:26** and **Deut 8:18**.

The bottom line is that your talent will make room for you and will bring you before kings if you are diligent in your business, which is His business. The Word says so in **Proverbs 22:29 Do you see a man diligent and skillful in his business? He will stand before kings; he will not stand before obscure men.** (AMP)

So whatever you do, do it with all diligence as unto the Lord. If you know His business and take care of it, He will take care of your business. That's what partners do for each other and that's what covenant is all about. That's what we call **CRM, C**rew (or **C**ockpit) **R**esource **M**anagement in aviation. It's called Team Work and it means using all available resources for a common cause.

CRM originated from NASA workshop in 1979. The workshop focused on improving air safety since there were findings indicating that primary cause for majority of aviation accidents were caused by human error, with main problems being *communication, leadership* and *decision making*. So, to avoid the human error and to improve our safety as we navigate in life, we must be able to use the correct *standard termi-nology* (the Bible vocabulary - speak the Word only), *acknowledge the only Leadership, God* as the Captain of our ship and make the *decisions only based on the Word of God.*

CRM training includes a wide range of knowledge, skills and attitudes including communications, situational awareness, problem solving, decision making, and teamwork. These are the same issues we deal in our lives. But be of good cheer, your Partner and Captain has provided for you your own Flight Standards Training Manual that includes this CRM training also. He wrote it for you. It is called the Bible! Refer to it often.

There's nothing stronger than the Blood Covenant and that's what we have with the Lord. He offered the partnership to us first and now we have the better end of the bargain. So take it, accept Him as your Captain! Join in business with Him. He has already paid the ultimate price for partnership with His blood.

Now, you be diligent in the part that He has offered for you to do and you, too, can be the one with the ten talents. After all, it is the Lord who promotes you when you are ready for the next step.

Airline Stuff

When you advance into Airline or Charter flying, you will have additional parts to the operation. For example, there are different departments and everyone has their particular purpose and job function so that everything can go as smoothly as possible. It is kind of like all of us in the Body of Christ have a special purpose and calling. If we all wanted to be a hand or an eye, then the body wouldn't function in its designed purpose.

Are you lonely?

Tired of working on your own?
Do you hate making decisions?

HOLD A MEETING!

You can –
• See people
• Show charts
• Feel important
• Point with a stick
• Eat donuts
• Impress your colleagues

All on company time!

MEETINGS

THE PRACTICAL ALTERNATIVE TO WORK

In commercial aviation operations there are departments like **Dispatch, Scheduling, Training Department, Recruiting** or **Human Resource Department** etc. Then there is the **Flight Operations Department**, which includes the **Flight Crew**, and things called Crew **Assignments** and **Rest Requirements** etc. These different parts will all work together as a whole in order for the operations to work as one.

First there's **Recruiting**, or **Human Resource Department**. Their function is naturally to select the Crew members to fly the assignments to be completed. This would be the calling you have and God is the Head of the Recruiting Department in the Heavenlies.

Then there's the **Training Department**. They will be in charge of completely training the Crew to meet the challenges and have the knowledge of everything they need to know to function as the Crew. This would be the Holy Spirit, our Teacher and Guide, who will train us and lead us on how to do the job we are called to do.

How about **Scheduling**? Their function is simply to give the Assignments to the Flight Crew. They will attempt to co-ordinate an efficient usage of available Crew resources to complete as many assignments as possible. They will also do the calling for the Crew

Members should there be a change of Assignments or need for Reserve Crew (those who are ready and standing by to be called). This, of course is the prompting of the Holy Spirit as He is leading us or calling us in a new direction.

The **Rest Requirements** have to do with rules relating to Crew Rest. Just like God said we should work six days and keep the seventh as the Sabbath, a day of rest, there are such rules in commercial aviation as well. The Airline I used to work for had exactly this rule that you could not be assigned for flight duty for more than six days. The seventh you must keep as the day of rest. There are also rules regulating how long you may be on duty continuously until you must be assigned time of rest.

These are important rules for safety in aviation as you can imagine. But, they relate to our lives more than we realize sometimes. You see, this same way Jesus withdrew away from the crowds to pray and spend time alone with God, so He would be able to continue hearing from the Father and be able to do what He was called to do after He was refreshed.

The function of **Dispatch** is to plan the flight routes, altitudes, planned fuel usage, check and update the latest weather and create a dispatch release with all of that information in it. They will then provide that information to the Flight Crew and work closely with them as they will be responsible together with the Crew for the safety of flight. This is part of the CRM we talked about previously, using all available resources for one common cause. Also, all parties will have to agree that the route and weather is acceptable for flight to depart and to reach the destination safely and that the fuel is sufficient.

Finally, the **Flight Crew** is the **Operations Department**. That's us working for God to further the Gospel, flying where ever the Assignment may take us, willing and obedient to answer the call.

CHAPTER NINE

Wisdom Nugget #9

Identify the signal you are
receiving. Make sure you
are tuned into the right
station. If you hear a
wrong message, it's
not the right source.

CHAPTER NINE

Trust, Be Willing and Obedient

Have you ever noticed that every so often there are words or subjects that just keep coming up in front of you everywhere you look. Those are seasons for those particular words and subject matters. I have noticed this on several occasions and I have learned to pay attention to such promptings and write them down as there is always a message behind them that the Lord is trying to get through to you.

One of such times happened not too long ago, when the Lord emphasized to me three words. They kept coming up in everything, whether it was me reading the Word or hearing someone preach. These words were trust, willing and obedient. They are still going on inside of me and the Lord is revealing more and more about these words as I write on these pages.

One of the first things the Lord pointed out was that the trust has to be there first before you can be willing and then comes obedience. Yes, you could obey reluctantly, but then there wouldn't be willingness and certainly no trust. If you trusted that someone has your best in their mind for you, you wouldn't be reluctant to obey them. So trust then makes you willing and therefore you obey for the right reasons.

If we really trust the Word of God, then there is no reluctance on our part to obey. We will be willing to do at any cost all what God is asking us to do as we *know* beyond the shadow of a doubt that it is to our benefit to do what the Word of God says, knowing that there is a reward at the end waiting for us. That's just how God works.

We can see this in aviation also, when our desire is to reach our destination, we depart in good faith that our resources will get us there safely. It doesn't matter if there's some rough weather on the way or not, as long as we have the right resources and no warnings from Flight Service Station or ATC of **dangerous** weather to avoid for the time being. So if we have the clearance that the flight is doable we will depart. That means that we have received what we have asked for. But, all have to agree in one. We must trust each other's judgment and know that if your departure is delayed it is because the ATC sees what lies ahead and that the delay is not denial. They are simply trying to protect you and get you out at the right time.

When you fly by the instruments, you trust they tell you the truth and you must trust that the Air Traffic Controller has your best in mind. When you trust, you are willing to obey and the reward is that all will be well at the end. You will get to your destination safe and sound, even if there was a rough ride or deviations due to weather in between your departure and your destination. You got there since you trusted, were willing and obeyed.

Your reward was always waiting for you, but the determining factor whether or not you got to see your destination was to listen to the directions and trust what the instruments and the ATC were telling you. Then when you obeyed, you lived to see the reward and got what you wanted and got to where you wanted to be.

The book of James in Chapter 1, verses 3 through 8 talks about this trust also. It mentions patient faith (trust), enduring that you may be perfect and lack nothing, with **nothing wavering**. That's how you get to your destination, even if you had to endure not so good weather on the way there. Through faith and patience you will receive the promise.

3 <u>Be assured</u> and understand that the trial and proving of your faith bring out <u>endurance and steadfastness and patience</u>.

4 But let endurance and steadfastness and patience have full play and do a thorough work, so that you may be [people] perfectly and fully developed [with no defects], <u>lacking in nothing</u>.

5 If any of you is deficient in wisdom, let him ask of the giving God [Who gives] to everyone liberally and ungrudgingly, without reproaching or faultfinding, and it will be given him.

6 <u>Only it must be *in faith* that he asks with no wavering</u> (no hesitating, no doubting). For the one who wavers (hesitates, doubts) is like the billowing surge out at sea that is blown hither and thither and tossed by the wind.

7   For truly, let not such a person imagine that he will receive anything [he asks for] from the Lord,

8   [For being as he is] a man of two minds (hesitating, dubious, irresolute), [he is] unstable and unreliable and uncertain about everything [he thinks, feels, decides].

— James 1:3-8 (AMP)

So, **in faith** equals revelation from God, hearing His Voice and **knowing** equals trusting that God is a giver, is always faithful and has your best in His mind. The double minded man simply has **not yet decided to trust God** and His Word. It is impossible to receive without trusting Him and His Word. The same way you cannot get to your destination if you are not trusting your instruments and obeying the ATC directions.

In Conclusion

Let's recap here what we have learned from aviation. First of all, you must **Trust your Instruments** and put some right input into you navigational instruments like your GPS so you know you are following the right signal. You must also tune and identify that you have the right frequency you are listening to. You must be **listening to the Right Voice** to get to your destination.

You also must **plan and prepare** before you take off. Otherwise the flight may not complete safely on the other end. You must be adequately prepared for your journey and along the way **use the right Words**.

Always keep in mind that the **Traffic Controller** has your best in mind. He is your Great Resource and has provided for you all that you need for you to get to your destination, so trust him.

When situations arise, use the **ADM** that your Training Department has taught you in order to make the best decisions in each situation.

Your **Attitude** is a major part in determining your Altitude. But, you also must add some **Power** to that Attitude with your **Words**. The Words in your mouth are like the gas in the tank. It keeps you powered up.

Now, you could be a glider and get some natural lift from outside source, like a thermal lift from a heated ground, but eventually that source cools off and you'll be gliding down. Your confessions of God's Word are like that engine that keeps you climbing as long as you put in some good gasoline into that tank (which is the Word of God in your mouth).

When you got your Words right, you may graduate to Jets and **High Altitude Flying**. This is where things accelerate and you are moving much faster than in the past. However, be aware of the **Aeromedical Factors Related to High Altitude Flying**.

Then there are some things that the enemy tends to try to do, and that is to get us **disoriented**, but if you **FOCUS** on God's Word you cannot be deceived. FOCUSing on God's Word will also work in defeating those **False Evidences Appearing Real**.

Always remember that God is feeding us spoon by spoon. He will lead us by **Levels of Learning**. When you are ready for the next step, He will offer you the promotion. Just learn to hear the **Voice behind the Word** and you will receive an **Avalanche of Blessings**.

Obey the Rules set in place. Obedience brings the Blessing.

Treat everything like **The Ten Talents** given to you. Give everything 100% and more and work as unto the Lord. Just like with the **Airlines** there are many components to the operations, in life also we are many parts of the Body of Christ joined together to do our part. Do your part with diligence for His Glory.

And finally, **Trust, be Willing and Obedient** and you will eat the Good of the Land.

(Isaiah 1:19)

My Prayer

My Prayer is that May God Richly Bless You and Yours as you have given to His Work through this book and May the Lord lead you in Your Designed Path of Life for His Glory.

About the Author

Tarja Newman has been attending Words of Life Fellowship Church in North Miami Beach, Florida since May of 1992. She is a licensed Airline Transport Pilot with Advanced Ground Instructor license and Gold Seal Flight Instructor ratings entitling her to teach Single-engine and Multi-engine pilots at all levels. Currently she is serving as an Assistant Chief Pilot at a local Flight School in South Florida. She has also worked as a crewmember in the airline industry and owned several businesses, but somehow her passion of teaching has always led her back into training others, both in aviation and in business.

Her passion in life is to find wisdom and pass it on to others as it relates to everyday life both personally and professionally. She credits all wisdom to the Word of God, which is the basis of her life and by which all things were created.

In the beginning was the Word...and the Word was
God...All things were made through Him...

— John 1:1-3

Then God said... and it was so.

— Genesis 1

Prayer of Salvation

If you are not absolutely sure and *know* that you are going to Heaven, pray this following prayer with me.

Dear Jesus, forgive me of all sins I have ever committed, knowingly or unknowingly. Come into my heart and lead me in the way that you designed me to walk in. Manifest yourself in me so that I may know you more real than this natural life and that I may know beyond a shadow of a doubt that when my mission here on earth is complete, I will live with you in Heaven forever.

In Jesus' Name I pray, Amen.

www.ingramcontent.com/pod-product-compliance
Lightning Source LLC
Chambersburg PA
CBHW061950070426

42450CB00007BA/1154